BODY ARTS
THE HISTORY OF TATTOOING AND BODY MODIFICATION™

THINK BEFORE YOU INK
Getting Tattoos

Nicholas Faulkner and Larry Gerber

Rosen
YA™
New York

Published in 2019 by The Rosen Publishing Group, Inc.
29 East 21st Street, New York, NY 10010

Cataloging-in-Publication Data

Names: Faulkner, Nicholas, author. | Gerber, Larry, 1946– author.
Title: Think before you ink: getting tattoos / Nicholas Faulkner and Larry Gerber.
Description: New York : Rosen Publishing, 2019. | Series: Body arts : the history of tattooing and body modification | Includes bibliographical references and index. | Audience: Grades 9–12.
Identifiers: ISBN 9781508180821 (library bound) | ISBN 9781508180838 (pbk.)
Subjects: LCSH: Tattooing—Juvenile literature. | Body marking—Juvenile literature.
Classification: LCC GN419.3 F38 2019 | DDC 391.6'5—dc23

Manufactured in the United States of America

CONTENTS

INTRODUCTION

The movies often portray getting a tattoo as a quick and spontaneous decision. A character walks into any old tattoo parlor and walks out a half hour later with perfect ink. But that's Hollywood. In real life, there are many factors to consider to avoid making what could become a costly and regrettable decision.

First, you have to ask yourself if you should get a tattoo at all. You're young and your tastes and values are changing all the time. What may seem important to you now may not be so important in the future. And getting a tattoo removed is costly, painful, and scarring. So in reality, once you get the tattoo, you'll be marked for life.

If you do decide to get one, the most important consideration is safety. Responsible tattoo artists take much of the same precautions against infection as doctors and dentists do. But there are other artists who don't. Does the artist makes a point of removing the new needle and tube setup from a sterile pouch while the customer is watching? Does the artist pour ink into disposable ink cups in front of the customer? Does the artist put on a new pair of disposable gloves before setting up tubes, needles, and ink? Is the artist will-

The decision to get a tattoo is an important one. There are many factors to consider, including safety, cost, and how you'll feel about your ink years into the future.

ing to answer questions about sterilization procedures, his or her safety record, and about his or her training in avoiding infections? The artist should also display or present upon request any state or city operating licenses and health board certificates.

Next, you need to decide which style of tattoo to get. Remember, you'll be looking at this design every day for the rest of your life. If you have something in mind, hang it up on your wall for a month and see if you get bored of it.

Are you looking for a traditional tattoo or an abstract decoration? "Traditional" is the name for the style of tattooing that became popular in the United States between World War I and World War II. Many military tattoos are examples of the traditional style. A few of the best known motifs are anchors, hearts, stars, roses, cartoons, and crosses.

Abstract tattoos sometimes have many possible meanings, depending on the intention of the wearer and the style of the tattoo. For example, ambigrams are graphic figures that mean the same thing—or sometimes the opposite thing—when they are viewed backwards, upside-down, or seen in a mirror. They may be words, images, or abstract designs. An ambigram may look like an angel in one view, but turn it upside down or look in a mirror, and the angel becomes a devil.

Fish designs are popular symbols in many cultures, and fish appear in many tattoo styles, including Celtic, religious, Native American, Polynesian, Asian, and many others. In Chinese tradition, the goldfish symbolizes good fortune, and the carp may represent wisdom and loyalty.

Dragons appear on tattoos around the world, but the dragon may mean different things in different places. In Europe and America, the dragon is traditionally a fearsome enemy who breathes fire and is battled by a brave warrior. In Asia, the dragon is more friendly and is often viewed as a force for good.

Flowers may represent life, death, birth, rebirth, and many other ideas depending on the type of flower. The rose is especially significant in Western cultures, and the lotus has special meaning in Eastern cultures.

These are just a sampling of the endless variety of tattoos styles you can get, and they may have different meanings across cultures, among family and friends, and in different careers, so choose wisely. It's also important to carefully consider what you really want. What may be meaningful to you today may not be so a few years, or decades, from now.

Before getting a tattoo, just about everybody has questions. Here are a few of the main ones: What kind of design do I want? Where should it go on my body? How will people react to it? Will it hurt? What will I think of my tattoo years from now? How can I avoid getting an infection? How do I take care of my tattoo, especially when it's new? Many of these questions can be answered by experts. Some of the answers will be pretty much the same for most people. Others are more personal and can be answered only by the individual getting the tattoo. This book will help you address them.

CHAPTER 1

TO TATTOO OR NOT TO TATTOO: THAT IS THE QUESTION

The decision on whether to get a tattoo is an important one. After all, you'll have this marking on your skin for the rest of your life. So the question is not only whether to get a tattoo, but which one to get if you do decide to take the plunge. Your tastes and values will change as you age, so a symbol or design that you like or love today may seem trivial or ugly in your later years. Aside from these personal factors, there are other practical considerations.

Age is an important factor when considering a tattoo. In most US states, the legal age of adulthood is eighteen. People under the legal age may get tattoos in some states as long as they have a parent's consent. But in many states, it doesn't matter whether a parent agrees or not; the law forbids giving a tattoo to anyone who's not an adult. For teenagers who want a tattoo, the laws might mean waiting a few months or a few years.

Don't be afraid to talk to your parents if you're considering getting a tattoo. They have a wealth of experience, and you may need their legal consent if you're under eighteen.

That leaves plenty of time to think about the decision, and there's plenty to think about.

Some people obey laws that they feel are more important than government regulations. Many Christians, Jews, and Muslims believe God's law forbids tattoos for people of any age. They often point to the Book of Leviticus, Chapter 19, verse 28, in the Old Testament or Torah. It says, "You shall not make any cuts in your body for the dead nor make any tattoo marks on yourselves: I am the LORD" (according to the American Standard Version of the Scripture).

Some people say that scripture verse doesn't apply to modern tattooing. They believe that the scripture was meant to discourage people in Biblical times from cutting themselves to mourn loved ones who had died, which was a custom of some ancient pagan religions in the Middle East. Many Christians and Jews believe that the commandment was intended to set true believers apart from unbelievers, not necessarily to ban the kind of body markings and decorations typified by modern tattoos. Faithful people who get tattoos don't feel they are breaking a commandment. They may even have tattoos of religious symbols or Bible verses.

Others insist that God does indeed forbid tattoos. In the Islamic religion, the law is often clearer than it is for Christians and Jews. Many Islamic teachers say those who get tattoos and those who give them are cursed.

WHAT PEOPLE WILL THINK

What about the person who has parental permission for a tattoo and who has no moral or religious problem with it? Is there any reason for him or her to consider what other people think about tattoos? It may not seem fair, but the answer is usually "yes."

Right or wrong, some people still look down on tattoos. This might not seem important now, especially if friends and family members have tattoos or if most of the people we know think tattoos are cool. But sooner or later, the opinion of someone who doesn't know us is going to make a difference in our lives.

Let's say a boss is choosing between two equally qualified applicants for a sales job. The boss likes both candidates. One has a tattoo on his or her hand, and the other doesn't. Even if the boss likes the tattoo, he will probably worry about what customers would think of it. In this case, the tattoo is a definite disadvantage.

Tats might also make a difference to a prospective boyfriend or girlfriend, or to that person's family. It's hard to predict the sort of people we'll meet in the future or to know what they'll think about our tattoos.

Health may also be at least a temporary, short-term consideration. Tattoo professionals warn that people with certain physical conditions shouldn't get inked. To avoid infection, those with open sores or lesions should wait until the problem is cleared up before having work done on their skin. Pregnant women should wait until they have their babies before they get tattoos. People who take blood-thinning medications should avoid tattooing as the breaking of skin could lead to excessive bleeding in these cases. Getting a tattoo isn't a good idea for anybody who's sick, even if it's just a cold. Some tattoo artists will refuse to work on people who have coughs or sniffles and will tell them to come back when they're healthy again.

CONSIDER YOUR REASONS

So far we have looked mostly at reasons for not getting tattooed. Now let's consider possible reasons in favor of it. Ask yourself, why do I want a tattoo? Are the reasons good ones?

1. **My friends are getting tattoos:** Are you feeling pressured to get a tattoo because your friends are also doing it? For some people, peer pressure can seem overpowering. But as kids grow up, they often get new friends or move to new places. What looks cool to people now in one school or in one town might still look cool years from now, someplace else. Or it might not. A tattoo might help us feel like we fit in with one group of people, but it might also make us feel awkward or embarrassed around another group later in life.

Peer pressure may be one reason why you want a tattoo, but think hard about the factors influencing your decision and whether they'll be important to you in the future.

2. **Celebrities, musicians, and athletes have tattoos:** Are there people you admire who have tattoos? Many movie stars, music stars, athletes, and other celebrities like to show off their tats. However, trends and tastes change over the years and what's hip today will eventually be outdated. Meanwhile, our tattoos stay the same.

3. **Tattoos can be tokens of commitment to girlfriends or boyfriends or tributes to family members and friends.** Many people get tattoos with names of boyfriends or girlfriends, along with symbols for love or friendship. Unfortunately, those relationships aren't always as permanent as the tattoo. One of the main reasons people go though the pain and expense of getting a tattoo removed is that they have broken up with someone.

   But some relationships do last forever. Casey, a music teacher in Oklahoma, has a tattoo of a baby's handprint on his chest. It's a tracing of his son's hand, and he got it right after the baby was born. Susan, who lives in California, especially loved her grandfather. After he died, she had his name and a personal reminder of him—a cowboy hat—tattooed on her shoulder.

4. **Tattoos can celebrate membership in a group of some kind and provide a sense of pride and belonging.** Many members of clubs, sports teams, bands, college fraternities and sororities, and the

(Continued on the next page)

(Continued from the previous page)

armed services get inked to remind them and others of their "tribe." Is group membership a good reason to get at tattoo? To answer that question, it may help to ask other questions: Will I always be a member of this group? If not, will I always want a reminder that I belonged to the group?

Many people can answer yes to those two questions, and they're happy with their tattoos. For example, there's a saying about the US Marine Corps: "Once a Marine, always a Marine." Many people who

Tattoos often celebrate membership in a club or an organization, showing unity and kinship among the group. Many military tattoos show allegiance to people's service.

served in the corps, as well as other branches of the armed forces, are proud of their military tattoos even though they are no longer on duty. The Marine Corps motto is "*Semper Fidelis*," meaning "Always Faithful," and many Marines feel that a permanent tattoo denoting membership in the Marines is an apt symbol of that faithfulness.

On the other hand, the Marine Corps has rules against excessive tattoos, such as "sleeve" tattoos that cover the entire arm or forearm, and other large tattoos that aren't covered by a uniform. Marines with sleeve tattoos can't apply for officer training.

WHAT WILL YOUR OLDER SELF THINK?

Members of organizations sometimes leave in anger or disagreement. If they have a tattoo symbolizing their membership, they may regret having to wear a permanent reminder of the group. Tattoos, often crude-looking homemade letters and symbols, are also popular among many street, bike, and prison gangs. But if members give up gang life, they may wish they didn't have the gang tattoo.

Thinking about a tattoo means thinking about the future as well as the present. That's not always easy

It's important to think about how you, and others, will view your tattoo in the future. What looks rebellious today as a young person may send a different message to the world when you're an adult.

to do. If something seems like it's important or a lot of fun in the present moment, we tend to think that it will always feel important or fun. But as time passes, people change, as do their attitudes. Some people simply outgrow their tattoos and get tired of them as they get older.

Tattoos are permanent. That's why it's important to take time and do some hard thinking before deciding whether to get a tattoo. If the answer is, "No, I don't want a tattoo," then that's the end of the questions. If the answer is, "Yes, I do," the questions are just beginning.

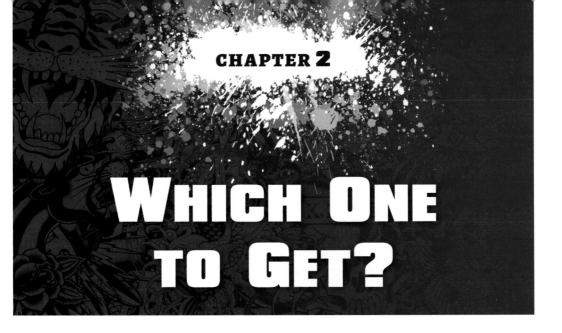

CHAPTER 2

WHICH ONE TO GET?

I f you do decide to get a tattoo, the next most important question is which one to get. There are literally endless choices. You can get one that's already established, such as "flash," which are ready-made designs on the walls of tattoo parlors. Or you can get a unique design. But when you decide what to get, think about what will be meaningful to you throughout your life, not just today. When considering what and where and how big, it helps to keep in mind the same questions we asked about getting a tattoo in the first place: What will I think of it years from now? What will other people think when they see it?

WHERE WILL IT GO?

Face, neck, fingers, hands, and forearms: tattoos on those parts of the body will usually be seen no matter what kind of clothes you wear. Anybody considering a tattoo on one of those spots should probably think very

You might consider getting your tattoo on an ankle, or some other inconspicuous area where you can easily conceal it if necessary at a job interview or a formal event.

hard about it. Tattoos in those places will be seen by just about everybody with whom one comes into contact. On the other hand, tattoos on the back, chest, and shoulder are often covered up by clothing. They probably wouldn't be seen by a job interviewer or by anyone else in a position to judge a person on the basis of appearance.

Body placement also affects the design and size of a tattoo. An artist would obviously have trouble tattooing an intricate design or a long quotation on somebody's hand or finger. And a tiny picture or symbolic letter might look strange tattooed all by itself on the expanse of someone's back or chest.

The bigger the tattoo, the more room there is for detail in the design. Bigger tattoos are also likely to make bigger impressions—for better or for worse—on people who see them. How big is big? The Marine Corps, which has the strictest tattoo regulations of any of the armed forces, doesn't allow visible tattoos bigger than a man's hand.

Placement on the body not only determines how visible a tattoo is to other people, but it also affects the way tattoos age. The look of the ink will change as the skin gets thinner and more wrinkled. Tattoos on parts of the body that move a lot, such as hands and fingers, usually fade and wrinkle sooner than tattoos on other parts of the body. If a tat is in a spot that's usually covered with clothing, it won't fade as much as a tattoo that's usually exposed to the sun's ultraviolet light.

Some parts of the body hurt more than others when they're being tattooed. Areas where the skin is thin or close to joints or bones are more painful. People with lots of tattoos say the most painful places are the lips, spine, feet, ankles, chest, ribs, elbows, the inside of the wrist, behind the ear, and around the eyes. The least painful places are the shoulders, arms, and thighs.

A UNIVERSE OF DESIGNS

Many modern tattoos are inspired by designs that are thousands of years old. They are taken from peoples and cultures around the world. Here is a look at some of the tattoo styles that have been popular in recent years.

- Celtic designs are intricate knots and mazes, usually done in black or blue ink only. They are inspired by centuries-old pieces of Celtic art and craftwork, particularly those found in Ireland. Celtic designs are more difficult than others to tattoo. It's recommended that customers who want a Celtic tattoo find an artist who specializes in them.

- Asian or Oriental is a broad category of tattooing that encompasses many cultures and traditions, including Japanese and Chinese tattoo styles. Many people favor simple tattoos of Japanese or Chinese text characters, while others decorate their entire bodies with symbolic carp, dragons, blossoms, and other decorations in the Japanese style.

Many tattoo styles have deep historical roots that go back centuries or even millennia. Celtic and Polynesian designs are just a couple examples of these ancient traditions.

- Polynesian tattoos—inspired by the island cultures of the Central and South Pacific—had a strong influence on modern tattooing. The word "tattoo" comes from the language of Tahiti, one of the islands in French Polynesia. Sailors who traveled in the Pacific during the Age of Exploration introduced Polynesian-type tattoos to Europe and America. Tahitians, Hawaiians, Maoris of New Zealand, Samoans, Tongans, and other native island peoples all have their distinctive styles.

- Native American designs figure in many modern tattoos. The best-known style is called Haida, the tribal name of a people in western Canada and southeastern Alaska.
- Tribal tattoos may resemble Polynesian or Native American designs, but they are often made up of abstract lines and swirls rather than images of specific things. Most of them are done with black or blue ink only.
- Traditional tattoos are usually inked in bold lines and bright colors. They include classic images like an anchor or a heart with "Mom" written on a scroll that is draped across the heart. The traditional style is thought to have started on US military bases after World War I.
- Military tattoos include symbols of a service branch, such as an aviator's wings for the Air Force or the eagle, globe, and anchor of the Marine Corps. US Army veterans often choose a replica of their unit patch, while Navy and Coast Guard veterans may

pick tattoos featuring ships or anchors. Men and women in all services frequently get tattoos honoring comrades killed in action.

- Religious styles of tattooing may include crosses, Bible verses, or Hebrew letters representing words that are important to the wearer.

- Biomechanical motifs were inspired by illustrator H. R. Giger, who designed the creature from the *Alien* movies. They usually show muscles intertwined with machine parts.

Traditional tattoo styles, such as the heart or the anchor, have stood the test of time. They may be a good option if you're going for a classic look that will be in fashion for decades.

- Biker tattoos often feature motorcycles, wheels, flames, women, skulls, and motorcycle gang logos.
- Gothic tattoos may be bats, vampires, or other "spooky" images.
- Black-and-gray is a tattooing style that is thought

to have originated in prisons, where artists couldn't get colored inks and instead used ink made from ashes or other available material. Professional black-and-gray tattooing features subtle shading, which requires a lot of skill by the artist.

- Realistic tattoos, also called portrait or photographic tattoos, also require special artistic skill and experience. They are usually done in black-and-gray, and they often look just like photographs or paintings.

EXPRESS YOURSELF

For many people, tattoos are a form of individual expression, so it makes sense for them to want an image that's unique, even one that they have designed themselves. Customers can take their own drawing to an artist, who helps them refine the idea and sketch out a design that can be tattooed.

Designs that include names have been popular for a long time, but many artists are reluctant to tattoo the name of a friend, boyfriend, girlfriend, or even a wife or husband. They worry that the relationship will not last, and that the wearer will come to regret getting the tattoo. The wearer's own name, as well as names honoring parents, grandparents, children, brothers, sisters, and loved ones who have died are safer because the importance and meaning of those relationships are less likely to change negatively over time.

If you have a custom design in mind, you can bring a sketch of it to the tattoo artist. He can then work with you on refining it to your liking.

THE POWER OF AN IMAGE

Unlike words, images can mean lots of things, depending on who's looking at them. Traditional flash pictures include hearts, anchors, butterflies, daggers, the Oriental yin-and-yang symbol, skulls, and stars. Custom images can be spectacular: scenes of heaven or hell, the face of a loved one or someone we admire, fountains, rockets, weapons, famous art works, bizarre creatures, elaborate abstract designs.

FINDING YOUR FONT

If a tattoo includes writing, the customer needs to decide on the font, or the style of lettering. There are hundreds of fonts to choose from, and the choice of font is an important decision. Some fonts make letters jump out at the viewer. Others make the lettering harder to read. Sometimes words are blended with pictures or designs, so that they can't be read at all without looking closely. Popular types of font include Gothic or blackletter styles (the best-known font in this category is Old English); Celtic or uncial lettering; graffiti, which includes many styles of modern writing as well as street scrawl; cursive handwriting, either the wearer's own style of script or one of many ready-made cursive fonts; Kanji, the Japanese version of Chinese calligraphy; and Hanzi, traditional Chinese writing. Other writing styles include icy and fiery, which aren't actual fonts but ways of making letters so that they look frozen or seem to be burning.

English and most other European lettering systems are based on the Roman alphabet. Other lettering includes Arabic; Sanskrit, an ancient language of India; Cyrillic, the alphabet of Russia and other Slavic countries; and the Chinese and Japanese systems. Some tattoo inscriptions are in made-up alphabets, such as the Elvish runes from J. R. R. Tolkien's *Lord of the Rings* trilogy. Examples of fonts and styles can be found on the internet or in the flash illustrations at tattoo shops.

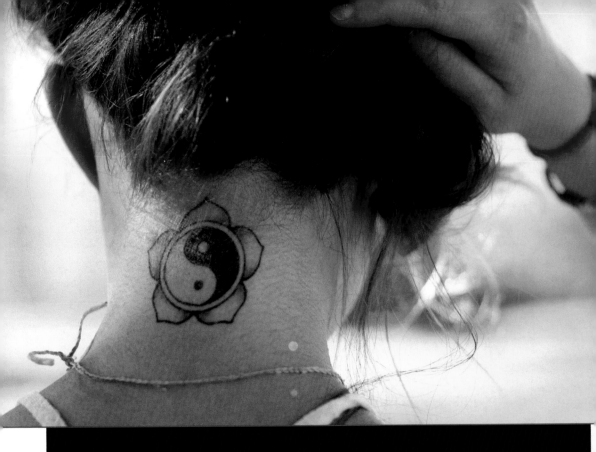

Universal designs, such as the yin-yang symbol, are easily recognizable across all cultures. They may also carry meaning that suits your personality.

Whatever sort of picture or design we choose for a tattoo, it's important to remember the two basic questions that must be asked throughout the decision-making process: Will I be happy with it years from now? What will others think about it?

Abstract designs are often safer than words or pictures of specific things, in terms of how we will think of them in the future and how others see them. To say something is abstract means that it doesn't depict a specific image. Abstract tattoos are usually intended to decorate a part of the body rather than to pass on a message. Many tribal designs are examples of abstract tattoo art. They may include bands circling an arm or a leg, strips or curls that flow with the natural curves of the body. They are sometimes done with color but more often in dark ink only.

Many Americans and Europeans who get tattoos choose Kanji or Hanzi characters because they look good as designs. Their meaning is clear only to the wearer and a few others. Because their meaning is obscure, Asian-character tattoos are often seen as special, exotic, or mysterious. Typical choices include the characters for strength, love, life, happiness, friendship, and other concepts. Other popular characters are signs of the Chinese zodiac, particularly those of the wearer's birth year: snake, dog, monkey, ram, rooster, and so on. Or the wearer may simply choose a character with a symbolic meaning he or she likes, such as a dragon, tiger, or cherry blossom.

CHAPTER 3

IT'S ALL ABOUT THE ARTIST

The only thing standing between you and a great tattoo is your tattoo artist. Finding the right person to do the job is critical, as there are a lot of unprofessional and, frankly, low-quality, tattoo artists out there looking to just make a quick buck. You want to spend a lot of time doing your research. Look for reviews online. Ask other people with tattoos for their recommendations. Don't just opt for the shop that's cheapest or near your home. Above all, you want a professional that works out of a safe and sterile environment.

Here are a few of the questions that need answers: Does the artist know how to ink the sort of tattoo I want? Have I seen samples of his or her work? What do other customers say? Is the artist a good listener? Does he or she answer all my questions? Do I get along OK with the artist? Do I feel comfortable in the shop? Is it safe and sanitary? Is there one main style that stands out in the artist's portfolio? It may also help to ask the artist what his or her favorite style is. Chances are, that's the style they're best at. But is it the style that you want?

TALK TO OTHERS

Finding the right artist often starts by first finding a happy customer. If someone is wearing a tattoo that looks appealing, ask who did the work and what the wearer thinks of the artist. Friends can give the most trustworthy advice about a particular artist or tattoo shop based on

Don't be shy. If you see someone with a tattoo that you like, ask her where she got her ink and which artist did the work. This is a great way to discover artists.

whether they've had a good experience or a bad one. The more people we ask, the more we learn.

At first, it may seem awkward to ask strangers or people we don't know very well, but most people like to talk about their tattoos and might even be flattered by the interest. Talking to customers not only gives a feel for what the artist is like, it's a chance to look at how the artist's work looks on real skin.

It's impossible to evaluate an artist without looking at his or her work. Many shops line their walls with pictures, and they may post a lot of pictures on their websites. But there's not always a way to be sure they are the actual work of the artist. Most reputable artists keep a photo album of their tattoos, and the portfolio usually has a signature or some kind of authenticating note that the samples were actually done by the artist.

When looking at the examples in the portfolio, check closely to see if the lines of the tattoos are smooth and clean. They shouldn't be shaky, jagged, or blurry. Lines should connect up where they're supposed to connect. Squares and circles ought to look really square and round, not distorted. Colored areas should usually look solid, and colored spaces should be filled in evenly. The tattooed skin in some of the example pictures might look red and puffy, but that's nothing to worry about. It's probably because the pictures were taken right after the tattoos were inked, before the customers left the shop.

All reputable tattoo artists have portfolios of their work. Look closely at the details, such as the accuracy of the lines, to make sure their skills match what you're looking for.

It's still possible to get an idea of the basic quality of the work. By looking at a lot of an artist's samples, a potential customer can also get a good idea of how much experience the artist has with the kind of tattoo that is desired.

It's wise to visit as many shops as possible before making a final decision. Professionals understand the uncertainty and anxiety that comes with getting a first tattoo. Real pros will be patient and friendly when it comes to answering questions and making customers comfortable. If they're not, it's time to look somewhere else.

THINKING ABOUT PRICE

Shopping around to find the best place to get a tattoo doesn't necessarily mean shopping around for the cheapest price. Experts warn against trying to get a bargain tattoo. Since tattoos are for life, quality work is much more important than trying to save a few dollars.

Tattoos are usually paid for by the piece or by the hour. Flash tattoos are usually a standard price, and often the shop's catalog of flash will include prices. In most places, a small stock design about two inches square will probably cost $100 or less and take about an

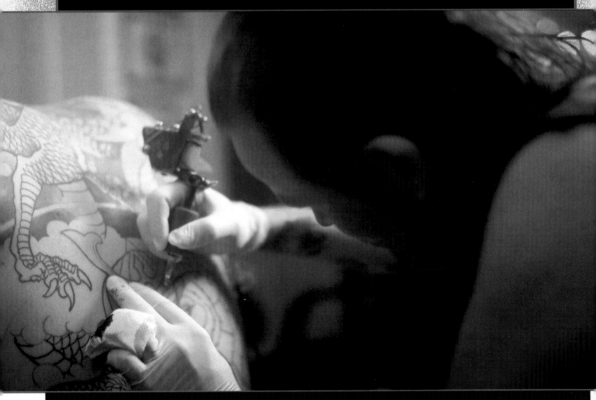

Price is a big factor when considering larger, more elaborate tattoo designs. The cost of detailed work that may take several visits can run into the thousands of dollars.

hour to complete. Prices vary a lot from place to place. Popular or well-known artists are usually more expensive than those who aren't so well known.

For larger tattoos, the artist will usually charge by the hour. Customers who bring their own designs can also expect to pay by the hour. Customers with limited funds can tell the artist how much money they have to spend and ask if it's possible to get the tattoo they want for that price. Once the artist quotes a price, it's not a good idea to try to bargain it down. Tattoo artists are professionals with their own standards, and they may take offense if someone seems to be trying to cheapen or devalue their work.

Tattoo artists, like most other service professionals, appreciate tips. Ten to twenty percent is the usual rate. And artists always appreciate it when customers recommend them to others.

Getting a tattoo should be fun. Finding an artist who's easy to talk to and pleasant to spend time with goes a long way toward making it an enjoyable experience.

SAFETY FIRST

Getting a tattoo should also be a safe experience. Since tattooing punctures the skin and draws blood, there's a risk of infection. When shopping for the right tattoo parlor, look around carefully to see if the place is clean. A shop may have funky décor and weird lighting, but it should never be dirty. And the area where tattoos are actually applied should have plenty of light.

The most serious health threat in tattooing is from blood-borne diseases. These include HIV, the virus that causes AIDS, hepatitis, and tetanus. Hepatitis is the biggest worry. Even a small scratch by an infected needle may transmit hepatitis, which can damage the liver. HIV can also be spread by infected needles or

A tattoo parlor should be a highly sterile environment, much like a dentist or doctor's office. Check to see if the tools are organized and sterile.

other implements that come in contact with human blood. However, HIV doesn't survive long outside the human body, and it isn't easily transmitted by tattoo needles. The Alliance of Professional Tattooists, citing information from the Centers for Disease Control and Prevention (CDC), says there haven't been any cases of HIV contracted by professional tattooing in the United States.

To reduce the risk of infection, all tattoo equipment must be properly used and sterilized. Anything that comes in contact with the skin or blood during the tattooing process should be either sterilized in an autoclave after use or put into a hazardous waste container for disposal. An autoclave is a machine that sterilizes needles and other equipment with high-pressure steam. If a shop doesn't have an autoclave, don't get tattooed there.

Most states have strict health regulations for tattoo shops, and operators are usually required to keep records of autoclave use, showing that their equipment is sterilized after each use. Shopkeepers should be happy to show their health and safety records to any customer who wants to see them, and it's always a good idea to ask. If a tattoo shop doesn't have up-to-date sterilization records, or if the staff seems reluctant to show them, then look somewhere else. While tattooing, artists should always wear disposable surgical gloves. Many artists, to be on the safe side, also get vaccinated for hepatitis. When talking to a prospective artist, it never hurts to ask whether he or she has been vaccinated.

All tattoo equipment is supposed to be single service. Needles come in sealed containers and are used only once. Then they are either sterilized in an autoclave or put into a sharps container for disposal. Ointments, gloves, razors, tubes, wipes, and liquids also get thrown away after use. They must be placed in hazardous waste containers, not in the regular trash can or the sink.

Since tattoo needles penetrate the skin, it's extremely important that the artist disposes of them immediately after each use to prevent the spread of disease.

Before tattooing, ink is placed in one-time-only caps that hold just enough for each tattoo. When the process is done, the containers are thrown away, along with any leftover ink. The leftover ink can't be used because it has come in contact with human blood.

Many states and cities require tattoo artists to get licenses or register with health authorities and to have regular inspections in their shops. Tattoo professionals may also be required to undergo health safety training. Look around to see if the shop displays licenses, health certificates, or state and/or city registration. If you're not sure what the regulations are in your area, ask. Artists and staff should have no problem giving details about their training, experience, and safety procedures.

Beware of scratchers. That's the term for someone who doesn't have formal training but provides tattoos anyway. Scratchers may work in homes, basements, or garages, often using a cheap tattoo kit. Many scratchers fail to sterilize and maintain their equipment properly, and many of them save money be reusing needles and other equipment. This is very dangerous for the risk of infection and deadly disease it poses.

CHAPTER 4

GETTING INKED: HOW IT WORKS

I f you've made the decision to get a tattoo, it's important to know what to expect on the big day. It may not be like it is in the movies where you can just walk into a tattoo parlor and come out a half hour later with a perfect and finished design. You'll likely have to set up an appointment. Don't just drop in without a reservation, expecting to get the tattoo and the artist you want when you want them. Tattoo artists are very busy professionals with many clients. Also, depending on the size and complexity of your tattoo, you may need to come back for several visits. And when it's done, you'll need to take proper care of it for a while to prevent infection.

Before going to the shop, it's important not to take aspirin or any other medication that thins the blood. Alcohol does the same thing. Alcohol and blood thinners can inhibit clotting and cause heavier bleeding. There will be some bleeding when the tattooing starts because

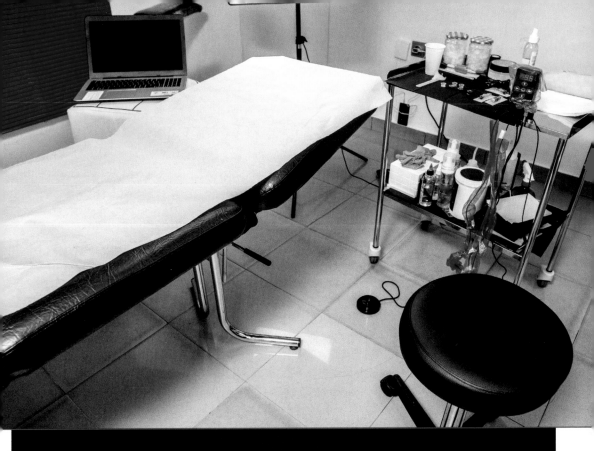

When it's time to get the tattoo, you'll recline on a chair or table in a relaxed position so the artist can comfortably do his or her work.

the skin will be broken, but excessive bleeding can hamper the tattooing process and increase the chances of receiving an inferior tattoo. Excessive bleeding is also a health risk.

It's a good idea to be rested up and to have eaten some food. People who are tired or who have low blood sugar may experience more discomfort or even faint.

When it's time for the work to start, the customer will be taken to the tattoo chair, usually in a separate room or section of the shop. Some tattoo artists use dentist chairs or recliners. Some studios just have regular chairs. The artist may ask if it's OK for someone else to watch the work, usually somebody who's considering getting a tattoo and wants to know how the process works before committing.

To begin the preparation, the artist will put on latex gloves and scrub the skin with alcohol or some other cleaning agent. Then the tattoo area is shaved. The artist should use a new, disposable razor. Shaving is important because otherwise the needle may push hair under the skin, thereby increasing the risk of infection.

Next, the design will be drawn on the skin to give the artist a guide to follow when applying the ink. Sometimes the design may be drawn directly onto the skin, but most often the artist will use a stencil. The skin area is then coated with deodorant, alcohol, or soap to make the transfer easier and leave clear lines. The stencil stays on for a minute or so to let the design transfer. When the artist removes the stencil, he or she will probably ask the customer to check the design in the mirror to make sure it's straight and in the right place. If it doesn't look right for any reason, now is the time to say so. This is the last chance to make adjustments. It's also the last chance to back out of getting the tattoo. It's fine to change your mind at this point. A professional tattoo artist will understand and respect your decision.

THE POINT OF NO RETURN

When it's time to start inking, the artist will pour the pigments from large storage containers into small ink cups, also called ink caps. The thimble-sized containers hold enough ink for one tattoo, and they are thrown away after a single use. The artist will open a sterile pouch of needles and tubes. This autoclave pouch has a dot that changes color to show the equipment inside has been sterilized. The pouch should be unsealed in front of the

Before the tattooing begins, the artist will pour the pigments that will be used in your design into small cups called ink caps.

customer. The artist will then assemble the tattoo equipment, turn on the machine, and get ready to apply the tattoo. Some people dislike the buzzing sound that the tattoo machine makes—it sounds sort of like a dentist's drill—and they come prepared with ear buds or headphones to drown it out.

The first step in applying the tattoo is doing the outline. This part usually hurts worse than the coloring and shading that come later. Pain tolerance varies from person to person. Some people say tattooing doesn't hurt much at all. Others compare it to a sunburn, a bee sting, a cat scratch, or even a cigarette burn. It's important to relax. Tensing up will just make the pain worse. The artist may use just a single needle for a thin line or a set of several needles for thicker areas. Multiple liner needles are usually arranged in a circle.

The first few lines usually hurt the most. If someone is getting a first tattoo, the artist will usually pause after the first strokes to see how the customer is doing. If he or she is queasy or faint, the artist will probably stop a minute to let the customer take some deep breaths before continuing. If the discomfort gets to be too much at any time, there's nothing wrong with asking the artist to stop for a minute to allow a stretch or a bathroom break.

As the artist inks the outline, using thin ink, he or she will stop the machine from time to time to wipe away the transfer ink and any blood. Artists usually work from the bottom up, so they don't smear the stencil outline. When the outline is finished, the artist will remove any remaining traces of transfer ink and clean the tattoo.

The next stage involves shading and coloring. The needles will have to be changed, so this might be a good time for a break. Using a variety of needles and a thicker ink, the artist goes over the design making clear, solid lines. The needles, known as shaders, may be set in a straight line, like the teeth of a comb. The tattoo is cleaned again before color is applied. Color inking can be uncomfortable, but it's usually not as painful as the outlining.

When applying color, the artist makes each line overlap so there are no holidays, or spots where color is missing. After inking, the artist cleans the area again with a disposable towel, then puts a sterile bandage on it. Bleeding usually stops a few minutes after the process is finished. How long the entire tattooing process takes and how many visits are needed depends on the size and intricacy of the tattoo.

TAKING PROPER CARE

Many shops will give the newly tattooed customer a pamphlet on caring for the tattoo. It's important to follow the precautions listed there and use proper care to keep the tattoo from fading, getting distorted, or getting infected. Here are some common guidelines for taking care of a new tattoo:

TOOLS OF THE TRADE

What's actually happening when an artist inks a tattoo? He or she is using an electrically powered "gun" that moves a needle up and down from fifty to 3,000 times a minute. The needle punctures the skin about one millimeter (0.04 inches) deep each time it goes down, leaving a drop of ink behind. The artist regulates the machine with a foot pedal, much like a sewing machine pedal.

Most tattoo inks aren't really inks at all, but various kinds of pigments in a disinfecting solution that spreads

The reason why tattoos are permanent is because the tattoo needle rapidly (up to thousands of times per minute) deposits the pigment deep under the skin.

the colors evenly. Manufacturers aren't required to reveal what's in their pigments, and the contents are usually regarded as a trade secret. They aren't regulated by the US Food and Drug Administration (FDA).

Most pigments are mineral based, while others are vegetable based or plastic based. Some of them, especially the colored ones, can cause allergic reactions. Red and yellow cause the most reactions. Some pigments glow in the dark or are visible only under ultraviolet light. These pigments have a risky reputation. While some of them are safe, others may cause radiation poisoning or other toxic reactions.

1. Remove the bandage when recommended, usually one or two hours after the procedure.
2. Wash the tattoo two or three times a day for the first week, using cool or lukewarm water and a mild antibacterial soap.
3. Don't soak the tattoo in water for a long time or put it directly under the shower.
4. Pat it dry. Don't rub!
5. Don't let clothing or anything else rub or irritate the new tattoo. If the tattoo is on an ankle, it might be good to avoid wearing socks for a while. If it's on the small of the back, make sure the waistband of your pants don't chafe it.

Caring for your tattoo soon after you get it is almost as important as choosing the right artist. Without proper care, your tattoo can get distorted or infected.

6. When applying antibacterial ointment, put on a very thin coat and gently work it into the skin. Too much ointment might take color out of the tattoo.
7. After three or four days, start using unscented lotion rather than antibacterial ointment to keep the tattooed skin moist. Don't use petroleum jelly, products with aloe, or anything that clogs the pores. The tattoo needs to breathe.
8. Keep the new tattoo out of direct sunlight and stay out of the swimming pool until it's healed. Sun and chlorine can fade tattoos.
9. There will probably be scabs. Let them heal natu-rally and fall off. Don't pick at them. If the skin itches, slap it lightly or apply more lotion. Don't scratch.
10. Call a doctor if there's any sign of infection. Signs of infection include red or puffy skin and tenderness to the touch. If a tattoo is healing properly, it won't be very painful to the touch after three or four days.

In general, follow the advice of the person who gave you the tattoo. Professionals know about aftercare and want their customers to be happy with their tattoos. For the first two or three days, blood, body fluids, and ink may continue to seep out of the tattoo. This is normal. During this time, most people wear clothes that they don't mind staining, and they may put a cloth on the bed at night to keep stains off the sheets. With proper care, the tattoo should heal in three to six weeks.

THE REMOVAL PROCESS

Most experts say it's impossible to completely remove every trace of a tattoo, but several newer methods of laser removal work better than methods used in the past. It's hard to predict how many traces of a tattoo will remain after removal, mostly because it's partly determined by what kind of ink was used initially. There are dozens of kinds of tattoo ink.

Other factors that affect how well a tattoo can be removed include placement, size, and how long it has been in place. It is often harder to remove a new tattoo than an old one. Tattoos done by good professional artists may be easier to remove, because the ink is likely to be more even.

Laser surgery is the most effective way to get rid of a tattoo. The laser penetrates the skin and breaks up tattoo pigments so they can be carried away naturally by the body's immune system. It may take several laser treatments, each about three weeks apart, to get rid of a tattoo. Black is the easiest color to remove because it absorbs more of the laser waves. Green and yellow are more difficult to remove.

Laser surgery can be painful. Some people compare it to little dots of hot grease being applied to the skin. Laser surgery can also be expensive. Some treatments cost several thousand dollars. Other methods of

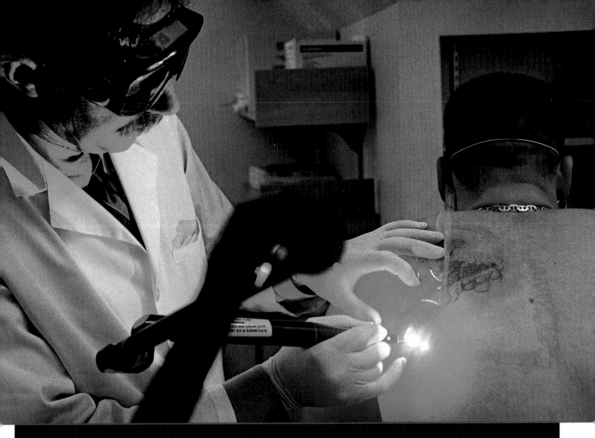

Though tattoos can theoretically be removed with lasers or other processes, the procedure often does leave permanent scars. It can also be costly and painful.

tattoo removal include dermabrasion, or sanding the skin; cryosurgery, or freezing the skin; and excision, cutting away the tattoo with a scalpel and stitching up the wound.

Traces of a tattoo almost always linger after tattoo removal. A tattoo, once applied, can never be completely erased. There will always be at least a partly visible remaining ghost mark or image where the tattoo once was.

Since tattoos are forever, think hard about the decision to get one. Consider future scenarios that involve how people will view your tattoos. Think carefully about the image or words you want tattooed and where you want to have them tattooed. Do research about the best and safest artists and shops in your area. This way, whether you ultimately opt to tattoo or not to tattoo, you can be happy, secure, and comfortable with your decision.

GLOSSARY

AIDS Acquired immune deficiency syndrome; a serious disease that's usually transmitted through contaminated needles, sexual contact, or blood products.

AUTOCLAVE A machine that sterilizes equipment using high pressure steam.

BIOMECHANICAL A style of tattoo art that shows human muscles mixed with machine parts.

CALLIGRAPHY An artful way of drawing letters or characters.

CELTIC Referring to an ancient people of Europe whose culture survives in Ireland and parts of Great Britain, Spain, and France.

CHINESE ZODIAC A system of counting time in cycles of twelve years, with each year named for an animal.

FONT A set of print characters that share a specific style.

HEPATITIS An inflammation of the liver caused by a virus or a toxic substance.

HIV Human immunodeficiency virus; the virus that causes AIDS.

INTRICATE Having a lot of fine or complicated details.

LESION A wound or injury, especially on the skin.

OBSCURE Having hidden meanings; difficult to find, discover, or comprehend.

PIGMENT Coloring material; a substance that provides color.

POLYNESIAN Referring to the people and culture of the Central and South Pacific islands.

PORTFOLIO A collection of samples of an artist's work, usually contained within a book, large carrying case, or, increasingly, in digital format.

REPUTABLE Having a good reputation, trustworthy, reliable, legitimate.

SCRIPTURE Writing that is regarded as sacred by a religious group.

SLEEVE Tattooing that covers a person's entire arm or forearm.

STERILE Free of bacteria and other organic matter that can cause infection.

American Academy of Dermatology
930 East Woodfield Road
PO Box 4014
Schaumburg, IL 60168-4014
(866) 503-7546
Website: http://www.aad.org
The academy's website features a directory of derma-
   tologists and advice on getting tattoos on its website.

Canadian Public Health Association
404-1525 Carling Ave.
Ottawa, ON K1Z 8R9
Canada
(613) 725-3769
Website: http://www.cpha.ca/en/default.aspx
This nongovernmental public health association pub-
   lishes information about tattoo safety guidelines at
   http://www.cpha.ca/en/portals/hiv/prevention/faq08
   .aspx.

National Tattoo Association
   485 Business Park Lane
   Allentown, PA 18109-9120
   (610) 433-7261
Website: http://http://nationaltattooassociation.com
The association provides tattoo safety information,

news, contact information for professionals, and pictures of the work of member tattooists in the United States, Canada, and other countries.

Public Health Agency of Canada
130 Colonnade Road
A.L. 6501H
Ottawa, Ontario K1A 0K9
(844) 280-5020
Website: https://www.canada.ca/en/public-health.html
The agency's website includes reports on tattooing, blood-borne diseases including hepatitis and HIV, and other information.

Society of Permanent Cosmetic Professionals
69 N. Broadway St.
Des Plaines, IL 60016
(847) 635-1330
Website: http://www.spcp.org
The society provides information about cosmetic tattooing and a directory of professionals. The society also has a Canadian directory of tattoo professionals.

Abdoyan, Brenda. *Teach Yourself Henna Tattoo: Making Mehndi Art With Easy-To-Follow Instructions, Patterns, And Projects*. East Petersburg, PA: Design Originals, 2016.

Aitken-Smith, Trent, And Ashley Tyson. *The Tattoo Dictionary: An A-Z Guide to Choosing Your Tattoo*. Mitchell Beazley, 2016.

Ashcraft, Brian, and Hori Benny. *Japanese Tattoos: History, Culture, Design*. Tokyo, Japan: Tuttle Publishing, 2016.

Cummings, Joe, and Dan White. *Sacred Tattoos of Thailand: Unveiling The Magic, Power And Mystery of Thailand's Ancient Tattoos*. New York, NY: Marshall Cavendish, 2011.

Friedman, Anna F. *The World Atlas of Tattoo*. New Haven, CT: Yale University Press, 2015.

Hardy, Lal. *The Mammoth Book of Tattoos*. Philadelphia, PA: Running Press, 2009.

Kaplan, Michael, And Marisa Kakoulas. *Tattoo World*. New York, NY: Abrams, 2011.

Kwiatkowski, P. F., And Tom O. Mehau. *The Hawaiian Tattoo*. Honolulu, HI: Mutual Publishing, 2012.

Mifflin, Margot. *Bodies of Subversion: A Secret History of Women and Tattoo*. New York, NY: Powerhouse Books, 2013.

Munden, Oliver, and Jo Waterhouse. *The Tattoo Color-*

ing Book. London, England: Laurence King, 2012.

Smith, Trent, And Ashley Tyson. *The Tattoo Dictionary: An A-Z Guide to Choosing Your Tattoo*. New York, NY: Hachette Book Group, 2016.

Von D, Kat. *Go Big Or Go Home: Taking Risks In Life, Love, And Tattooing*. New York, NY: Harper Design, 2013.

BIBLIOGRAPHY

AAA Tattoo Directory. "Tattoo Regulations by State."
Retrieved September 2010. http://www
.aaatattoodirectory.com/tattoo_regulations.htm.

Alliance of Professional Tattooists. "Basic Guidelines for
Getting a Tattoo!!!" 2010. http://www.safe-tattoos.com.

American Society for Dermatologic Surgery. "Do's
and don't's when considering tattoos or piercings."
Retrieved September 2010. http://www.asds.net
/DosAndDontsConsideringTattoosPiercings.aspx.

Bjarnoson, Dan. "Skin Deep." CBC News Online. October 21, 2004. http://www.cbc.ca/news/background
/tattoo/skindeep.html.

Bloginity staff. "Kelly Osbourne Plans Tattoo Removal."
October 5, 2010. http://www.bloginity.com
/blog/2010/10/05/kelly-osbourne-plans-tattoo
-removal.

Centers for Disease Control and Prevention. "Can I get
HIV from getting a tattoo or through body piercing?"
March 25, 2010. http://www.cdc.gov/hiv/resources/qa
/transmission.htm.

Clerk, Carol. *Vintage Tattoos: The Book of Old-School
Skin Art*. New York, NY: Universe, 2009.

DeMello, Margo. *Bodies of Inscription: A Cultural History of the Modern Tattoo Community*. Durham, NC:
Duke University Press, 2000.

Discovery Health. "How Tattoo Removal Works."

Retrieved October 2010. http://health.howstuffworks
.com/skin-care/beauty/skin-and-lifestyle/tattoo
-removal.htm.

Gerwig, Pastor Chuckk. "Tattoo and the Bible." 2007.
http://www.sacredink.net/tattoo_and_the_bible.

Gilbert, Steve. *Tattoo History: A Source Book*. New
York, NY: Juno Books, 2000.

Gleason, Kathy. "Contraindications to Getting a Tattoo."
March 4, 2010. http://www.suite101.com.

Green, Terisa. *Ink The Not-Just-Skin-Deep Guide to
Getting a Tattoo*. New York, NY: NAL Trade, 2005.

Green, Terisa. *The Tattoo Encyclopedia: A Guide to
Choosing Your Tattoo*. New York, NY: Fireside, 2003.

Hardy, Lal. *The Mammoth Book of Tattoos*. Philadelphia, PA: Running Press, 2009.

Hesselt van Dinter, Maarten. *The World of Tattoo: An
Illustrated History*. Amsterdam, Netherlands: Mundu-
rucu Publishing, 2007.

Jewell, Fred, and Stan Schwartz. "How Does a Tattoo
Gun Work?" June 29, 2010. http://www.faqs.org/faqs
/bodyart/tattoo-faq/part8/section-5.html.

"Kat Von D Makeup Collection | Kat Von D Beauty." Kat
von D. Retrieved November 29, 2017. https://www
.katvondbeauty.com.

Krcmarik, Katherine L. "Choosing a Tattoo Artist/Stu-
dio." Michigan State University, 2003. https://www
.msu.edu/~krcmari1/individual/get_artist.html.

The L Magazine. "The 10 Greatest Misspelled Tattoos." July 7, 2008. http://www.thelmagazine.com /TheMeasure/archives/2008/07/17/the-10-greatest -misspelled-tattoos.

Lisbon, Gunnery Sgt. Bill. "Corps Clears Up Tattoo Policy." US Marine Corps, February 4, 2010. http://www .usmc.mil/unit/mcasyuma/Pages/20100204tattoo .aspx.

Mayo Foundation for Medical Education and Research. "Tattoos: Understand risks and precautions." February 16, 2010. http://www.mayoclinic.com/health /tattoos-and-piercings/MC00020.

Muslimconverts.com. "Ruling of Tattoos in Islam." Retrieved September 2010. http://www .muslimconverts.com/cosmetics/tattoos.htm.

Richards, Bailey Shoemaker. "How to Choose a Tattoo Artist." October 7, 2009. http://www.suite101.com /content/how-to-choose-a-tattoo-artist-a156709.

Tao of Tattoos. "Gang and Prison Tattoos." Retrieved September 2010. http://www.tao-of-tattoos.com /gangs.html.

"Tattoos." Smithsonian.com, January 01, 2007. https://www.smithsonianmag.com/history /tattoos-144038580/.

"Tattoos and Tattoo Art. tattoostattoo." Pinterest. Retrieved November 29, 2017. https://www.pinterest .com/tattoostattoo.

Tattoo Collection, The. "Choosing a Tattoo Artist."
Retrieved September 2010. http://www
.thetattoocollection.com/choosing_a_tattoo_artist
.htm.

U.S. Food and Drug Administration. "Tattoos & Perma-
nent Makeup." June 23, 2008. http://www.fda.gov
/Cosmetics/ProductandIngredientSafety
/ProductInformation/ucm108530.htm.

The Vanishing Tattoo. "Tattoo Facts and Statistics."
2003. http://www.vanishingtattoo.com
/tattoo_facts.htm.

Winkler, Kathleen. *Tattooing and Body Piercing Under-
standing the Risks*. Berkeley Heights, NJ: Enslow
Publishers, 2002.

Zjawinski, Sonia. "What to Expect When Getting a
Tattoo." *New York Magazine*, September 24, 2007.
http://nymag.com/guides/everything/tattoos/37979.

INDEX

ABOUT THE AUTHORS

Nicholas Faulkner is a writer living in New Jersey.

Larry Gerber, a former Associated Press correspondent and bureau chief, has been writing news and feature articles for more than forty years. His interest in tattooing began in 2000, when his daughter said she wanted to get a friendship tattoo.

PHOTO CREDITS

Cover, p. 1 Jen Petreshock/The Image Bank/Getty Images; p. 5 © iStockphoto.com/dstephens; p. 9 Steve Debenport/E+/ Getty Images; p. 12 © iStockphoto.com/Drazen_; p. 14 Mauricio Limo/AFP/Getty Images; p. 16 ballyscanlon/Digital Vision/Getty Images; p. 18 © iStockpoto.com/erlucho; p. 20 Gideon Mendel/ Corbis Historical/Getty Images; p. 22 Giulia Bertaglia/Moment/ Getty Images; p. 24 © iStockphoto.com/skynesher; p. 26 Rosmarie Wirz/Moment/Getty Images; p. 29 Hinterhaus Productions/DigitalVision/Getty Images; p. 31 Mel Melcon/Los Angeles Times/Getty Images; p. 32 Portra/E+/Getty Images; p. 34 Romona Robbins Photography/Image Source/Getty Images; p. 36 Patila/Shutterstock.com; p. 39 © iStockphoto.com/jgaunion; p. 41 David Tadevosian/Shutterstock.com; p. 44 Westend61/ Getty Images; p. 46 Mikhail_Kayl/Shutterstock.com; p. 49 Boston Globe/Getty Images; cover and interior background design (tattoo) GOLFX/Shutterstock.com.

Design and Layout: Brian Garvey
Photo Researcher: Karen Huang